PAIN.PROCESS.PURPOSE.

CHANEL CHASE

Copyright ©2017 Chanel Chase
Publishing Company: October 7th Publishing LLC

Address:
P.O. Box 1271
Mableton, GA 30126

All rights reserved. No part of this book may be reproduced or transmitted in any form or by any means whatsoever (electronic, mechanical, scanning, photocopy, recording, or any other form) without written permission from the author, except for brief quotations in a book review.

ISBN: 978-0-9994946-1-5

Cover Design: Tamlyn Design

Workbook Layout: Solex Enterprises, LLC

PAIN. PROCESS. PURPOSE.

I understand that you are buying this workbook because you have read my book, and I pray that my journey impacted your life. However, going through my journey was great, but now we need to dig through yours. The best part about your journey is that you are going to get through it, and we can get through this together. I have created some compelling questions for you to answer about your journey. I pray that you utilize this workbook and start journaling your way to your purpose. I don't expect you to rush through this process. This workbook was designed to help you heal and experience God's best for your life. Sometimes the hardest part is putting your feelings on paper. When you release your feelings from your spirit, it will be very therapeutic and helpful in your healing. The best part of this is that you will grow through your process. I did through mine, and you will too, but at your own pace. I hope it's clear to you now that if God created a purpose for me, then HE HAS ONE FOR YOU AS WELL!

How To Utilize the Workbook:
I have questions divided into 3 parts: Pain, Process, and Purpose. Within each section, I have relayed to you part of my story, but remember this workbook is primarily for YOU. I have added personal trinkets that have helped me in these categories. I absolutely want this to be about YOU and YOUR CHASE TO YOUR PURPOSE WITH GOD! There are also exercises that will allow you to think about your current journey and will stretch your mind and your relationship with yourself and God. I have allocating free writing space at the end of each part so you can write freely outside of the specific questions and exercises.

AS AN BONUS, I have added one of my personal favorites to the back of the book. When I was going through all of these parts in my life and as I'm still discovering and chasing my purpose, I've realized the journey God brought me through. Part of the reason I am able to see that is because I used a "Thank You Journal." Even in the midst of my pain, during my process, I'm living in my purpose, every day I find something to be thankful for. I may even just look over a situation that I went through and thank God for where I am now. You may do that often with this workbook. I pray that you truly utilize your "Thank You Journal" section. Write down the good, the bad, and the indifferent. God will see this, and honestly, you will see the growth in yourself by the time you are done with this workbook. This is my favorite part of the workbook, so please make sure you do utilize it. (Refer to page 97 to begin using your "Thank You Journal")

Love Always,
Chanel Chase

PAIN

Let's talk about pain. I referenced losing my identity, and that was a very painful situation for me. I felt lost. I felt alone. I was hiding behind the lies of happiness. I wanted to be happy, but I couldn't be. I didn't know how to be. I lost who I was with God. I didn't know what love was. I was searching for love. I lost myself in my mess. I want you to truly think about your pain. That was my pain, but how did you feel when you were reading it? If you utilized the free writing space in your book, reference back to your book and what you wrote after reading that section. I'm going to ask you some more questions, and I want us to work through them together.

1. How do you define yourself?

___

2. Do you feel good about yourself when you do a self-evaluation or are you ashamed of yourself?

___

3. If ashamed, what specifically brings you to shame? Be honest with yourself and God.

PAIN. PROCESS. PURPOSE.

Now, I have an exercise for you. I want you to write down 7 words that you feel define who you are. (You will need to use them later.)

PAIN . PROCESS . PURPOSE .

Great! I'm glad that you were able to be honest with yourself. Whatever the outcome was, the good thing is that you can still change that mindset. From reading through my story, I was honest with you about how I felt about myself. I didn't know who I was, but the best part is that I was learning to admit it. Congratulations! You passed the first step!! You truly dug deep and thought about your definition of yourself. When you come to terms with how you feel about yourself, then you can truly correct what needs to be corrected.

Do You Know What God says about you?

For you formed my inward parts; you knitted me together in my mother's womb. I praise you, for I am fearfully and wonderfully made. Wonderful are your works; my soul knows it very well. My frame was not hidden from you, when I was being made in secret, intricately woven in the depths of the earth. (Psalm 139:13-15 AMP)

Let's Reflect on what this verse means to you:

_____
_____
_____
_____
_____
_____
_____
_____
_____
_____
_____
_____
_____
_____
_____
_____

PAIN. PROCESS. PURPOSE.

You are FEARFULLY and WONDERFULLY made. I want you to think about that when answering this next question.

4. Would your reflection of yourself and God's reflection of you mirror each other or be completely different?

PAIN.PROCESS.PURPOSE.

If your thoughts are anything short of what God said, I'd like to try another exercise with you.

I have left two columns for you. On the left, write down your attributes of how you saw yourself in the previous exercise. You will want to use the same 7 words that you identified in the previous exercise. On the right, I want you to find a verse in the Bible that "supports" your descriptor. However, if it was negative like mine were in my book, I want you to find the opposite of your descriptor. (Example: If I had angry, I would look for a bible verse about being happy.) When that is done, I want you to realize everything that God told you that you are, and don't allow Satan to destroy that.

1. _____   1. _____
2. _____   2. _____
3. _____   3. _____
4. _____   4. _____
5. _____   5. _____
6. _____   6. _____
7. _____   7. _____

How did doing this exercise make you feel?

_____
_____
_____
_____
_____
_____
_____
_____
_____
_____

PAIN. PROCESS. PURPOSE.

Let's re-define your thoughts of yourself. I want you to think of some powerful *"I AM"* statements to define yourself from this day forward. Everything negative that you thought about yourself prior to today is OVER! New mindset, new you! Start professing victory over your life.

I am _____!

I am _____!

I am _____!

I am _____!

I am _____!

I am _____!

I am _____!

I am _____!

I am _____!

I am _____!

I am _____!

I am _____!

I am _____!

I am _____!

I am _____!

I am _____!

I am _____!

I am _____!

I am _____!

I am _____!

I am _____!

I am _____!

I am _____!

I am _____!

I am _____!

I am _____!

I am _____!

PAIN . PROCESS . PURPOSE .

Remember, seeds yield harvest. Paul states in Galatians 6:7, "Don't be misled—you cannot mock the justice of God. You will always harvest what you plant (NLT)." Here's your time to start planting good and bountiful seeds. Speak life into your life! You are planting seeds in your spirit that will birth right into your purpose. Take your *I AM* statements very seriously, and watch the harvest manifest in your life.

5. Did you have a point in your life where you felt like you were alone?

_____
_____
_____
_____
_____
_____
_____
_____
_____
_____

6. What do you think caused you to feel like you were alone? Take this time to really dig deep and be honest with yourself and God!

_____
_____
_____
_____
_____
_____
_____

PAIN. PROCESS. PURPOSE.

PAIN.PROCESS.PURPOSE.

For me, I felt alone because I forgot that God was with me. I forgot who I was and essentially that led to me feeling as if God had left me as well. During that time of my pain, it was hard for me to understand that God was still with me. I believe that everyone at some point will struggle with feeling alone. It may be because we feel like no one else understands our situations, or it may be just because of the phase of life we are going through. However, God's Word is the answer. He is the key to fulfilling our empty parts and making them whole again. It's important that we find our comfort in God. I'm going to share some verses with you that I used to remind me that God is always with me.

Be strong and courageous. Do not be afraid or terrified because of them, for the LORD your God goes with you; he will never leave you nor forsake you." (Deuteronomy 31:6 NIV)

So, do not fear, for I am with you; do not be dismayed, for I am your God. I will strengthen you and help you; I will uphold you with my righteous right hand. (Isaiah 41:10 NIV)

For the sake of his great name the LORD will not reject his people, because the LORD was pleased to make you his own. (1 Samuel 12:22 NIV)

Let's Reflect on what these verses mean to you:

_____
_____
_____
_____
_____
_____
_____
_____
_____
_____
_____
_____
_____

CHANEL CHASE

7. Think about your situation, did you cling to God during this time or did you push Him away? If you did push Him away, why do you think you did that?

PAIN . PROCESS . PURPOSE .

8. How do you think your answer to the previous question affected the trajectory of your situation?

_____
_____
_____
_____
_____
_____
_____
_____
_____
_____

9. What are the specific moments in life that you identify with pain? Be specific and write each and every situation that you identify pain with down. I will give you some extra room on this section because this is the question that is going to provoke some healing in your life.

_____
_____
_____
_____
_____
_____
_____
_____
_____
_____

PAIN. PROCESS. PURPOSE.

PAIN . PROCESS . PURPOSE .

10. What event caused you the most pain? How does it make you feel today when you think about it?

_____
_____
_____
_____
_____
_____
_____
_____
_____
_____
_____
_____
_____
_____
_____
_____
_____
_____
_____
_____
_____
_____
_____
_____
_____

PAIN . PROCESS . PURPOSE .

11. When have you allowed your pain to detour you from your purpose?

PAIN. PROCESS. PURPOSE.

12. Can you remember the moments during your pain where you could have improved your response? Taking self-responsibility for your role is vital to growth, so take some time and really be honest with yourself and God about every situation.

PAIN . PROCESS . PURPOSE .

Now, some of these questions probably made you dig a little deeper, and that's the goal. When I was dealing with my pain, it was so hard for me to answer some of these same questions. I know I didn't cling to God because I was mad at God. I know I got off the path He intended for me because I made my own decisions versus His decisions. The goal of this workbook is to help you think through all the feelings that we try to mask daily. The goal is to get to the bottom of your pain with God. The best thing about your pain is that when you give it to God, He will do the rest. Here are some verses you can focus on to remind you that God is always directing your path.

Your word is a lamp to my feet and a light for my path (Psalms 119:105 NIV).

You make known to me the path of life; you will fill me with joy in your presence, with eternal pleasures at your right hand. (Psalms 16:11 NIV)

He leads me beside still waters. He refreshes and restores my soul (life). He leads me in paths of righteousness for his name's sake. (Psalm 23:2-3 AMP)

In all your ways acknowledge him, and he will make straight your paths. (Proverbs 3:6 AMP)

All the paths of the Lord are lovingkindness and goodness and truth and faithfulness, to those who keep His covenant and His testimonies. (Psalm 25:10 AMP)

I am the light of the world. He who follows Me will not walk in the darkness, but will have the Light of life (John 8:12 AMP).

Let's Reflect on what these verses mean to you:

_____
_____
_____
_____
_____
_____
_____
_____
_____
_____

13. Now that you have found the moments of improvement, do you see places where God still comforted you even though you felt He wasn't there?

14. How do you view God's Love for you working in your life currently?

PAIN. PROCESS. PURPOSE.

Let's do a little exercise:

Remember the columns, we are going to try that again. On the left side, I want you to write down 7 words that define God's Love. On the right side, I want you to find a verse that supports your view of God's Love. If there are no supporting biblical verses, then evaluate why you chose that word for God's Love and if you can, find another word to replace it with.

1. _____
2. _____
3. _____
4. _____
5. _____
6. _____
7. _____

1. _____
2. _____
3. _____
4. _____
5. _____
6. _____
7. _____

I'm so happy that you took the time to do that. One of the main reasons it was important to me that you did that is to show you how deep God's Love runs. I know in my journey, I write about how I was angry at God and I didn't feel His Love, and I didn't know He was there. However, God was truly sparing me each and every day. He was watching over me even when I didn't feel I deserved it. That's LOVE. God's Love is amazing. Sometimes we overlook the small things in life that we tend to take for granted. God has always been with us and will continue to be with us forever and ever. Even if you feel like that pain defined you, it doesn't. Remember, you are defined by God. You are smothered in God's Love, and your pain is just a stepping stone to greatness.

15. Do you feel like you can let go of your pain and move forward toward your process? I also want you to write down the people that were hurt in the situation or that you hurt, and I want you to forgive them. This is essential for growth.

_____
_____
_____
_____
_____
_____

PAIN. PROCESS. PURPOSE.

PAIN. PROCESS. PURPOSE.

PAIN . PROCESS . PURPOSE .

Here's where we cry it out! Before you go to the next section, I need you to stop and just spend some time with God. Go pray and read your bible. In Joshua 1:8 the Bible states, "This book of the law shall not depart out of thy mouth, but thou shalt meditate day and night. And then I will make thy way prosperous, and then thou shalt have good success (KJV)." Feed the word into your spirt. I'm not sure what your pain was caused by. It could be a friendship, a relationship, a career loss, or a death. There are a plethora of situations that cause pain. But before you can move forward, you have to let go. Not just let go, but you have to forgive. In Ephesians 4:26-31 the Bible states, "In your anger, do not sin: Do not let the sun go down while you are still angry, and do not give the devil a foothold. Anyone who has been stealing must steal no longer, but must work, doing something useful with their own hands that they may have something to share with those in need. Do not let any unwholesome talk come out of your mouths, but only what is helpful for building others up according to their needs, that it may benefit those who listen. And do not grieve the Holy Spirit of God, with whom you were sealed for the day of redemption. Get rid of all bitterness, rage and anger, brawling and slander, along with every form of malice (NIV)." We can't hold on to the people that hurt us or that situation that tried to break us. So, before you go to the next section, make sure you have truly let go and given the pain to God. It may take you a couple of days to process through this section and that is okay. Just take your time, and trust God to prepare you for your process! As mentioned before, remember the back of the book has your "Thank You Journal" in it. Remember to consistently thank God for the small things He is doing even through your pain.

I'm going to leave you some blank pages so you can just journal before you move on.

MY PERSONAL THOUGHTS…

_____

_____

_____

_____

_____

_____

_____

_____

_____

PAIN.PROCESS.PURPOSE.

PAIN . PROCESS . PURPOSE .

PAIN . PROCESS . PURPOSE .

PAIN. PROCESS. PURPOSE.

PAIN . PROCESS . PURPOSE .

PROCESS

Let's talk about process. Everyone's process is different. Mine was about obedience, finding myself, getting through the trials, and learning how to spend alone time with God. The pain hurt, but the process was where I gained strength. Once you let go of the hurt, it leaves you in limbo land while you are trying to figure it out. It's kind of like a scrape. The pain trial is when you first get a scrape and its bleeding and very open. The process stage is when that scrape has healed to become a scab and you bump it against something and that scab begins to open and bleed a little. That's what process was to me. It was tiny bumps against that scab that opened different situations in life, but the scab eventually heals. I got through it with God and so will you. I pray that in your process you learn to get closer to God like I did. I learned that people may let you down, but God will always be there.

Love Always,
Chanel Chase

1. Have you acknowledged God through your process?

_____
_____
_____
_____
_____
_____
_____
_____
_____
_____
_____
_____
_____
_____

PAIN. PROCESS. PURPOSE.

2. How does your acknowledgment of God translate into your obedience to God?

PAIN. PROCESS. PURPOSE.

For me, my process was about finding God and really seeking Him. It's so easy to pull away from God when stuff goes opposite of how we want it, but our goal should be to draw closer. When I was going through this time in my life, every week, I would find 7 scriptures that would help me stay focused and write them down. I would meditate on those scriptures and make them apart of me. I'm going to give you some verses that I chose during my weekly studies and my personal evaluation of them.

1. In all your ways acknowledge Him, and He will make your paths straight. (Proverbs 3:6 AMP)

   My reflections: *This verse taught me that if I kept God at the forefront of my life and acknowledged Him, even in the midst of the storms, He would guide me. My goal during my process was to stay steadfast on God. Although you saw in my journey I made some mistakes, I tried to stay focused on acknowledging God and asking him to guide me.*

2. But seek first His kingdom and His righteousness, and all these things will be added to you. (Matthew 6:33 NKJV)

   My Reflections: *It went along the path of the other verse, but through this verse, I feel like God was telling me that if I keep God at the forefront, he would take care of me. He would add things to my life. When I think about adding things to my life, I think about production, fruitfulness, and multiplication. He will multiply my abundance. He will add the fruits of the spirit (love, joy, peace, happiness, longsuffering, ect), and he will give me a fruitful life. It all starts with acknowledging Him.*

3. Commit your works to the Lord and your plans will be established. (Proverbs 16:3 ESV)

   My Reflections: *Wow, this one just blows me out of the water. If we acknowledge God and commit the things that we do to God, then He has already established our plans. To me, this was confirmation. If I just trusted in God to give Him everything, I wouldn't have to worry. He would already have established my plans. The comfort of just knowing that allowed me to get closer and closer to God.*

4. Delight yourself in the Lord; and He will give you the desires of your heart. (Psalm 37:4 ESV)

   My Reflections: *When I read verses like this, I just get all happy inside. All I have to do is delight myself in the Lord, and God will give me the desires. So, I had to actually look up what delight meant. According to the Merriam-Webster Dictionary, "delight is a high degree of gratification or pleasure, extreme satisfaction." When I thought about that, it blew my mind away. All we have to do is give God a high degree of gratification, make sure he is in extreme satisfaction, and he will give us the desires of our heart. To me, this was another reason to make sure we acknowledge God in our situations.*

5. For from Him and through Him and to Him are all things. To Him be the glory forever. Amen. (Romans 11:36 ESV)

   My Reflections: *Everything that we do should always be through God. If we can train ourselves to give Him glory in the midst of every situation, then we are training ourselves to be successful. Acknowledging God is very important because everything we do should go through Him.*

6. But from there you will seek the Lord your God, and you will find Him if you seek Him with all your heart and with all your soul. (Deuteronomy 4:29 NKJV)

   My Reflections: *When we are going through our journeys with God, we have to remember that we need to seek Him always. We have to give him all of our heart and all of our souls, and He will do the rest. As we are going through our processes, it's important for us to reach towards God, giving Him all that we can.*

7. With all this going on for us, my dear, dear friends, stand your ground. And don't hold back. Throw yourselves into the work of the Master, confident that nothing you do for Him is a waste of time or effort (1 Corinthians 15:58 MSG)

   My Reflections: *We can't let anything move us. I had to choose to not allow my situations to determine my relationship with God. This was a hard journey for me, but I had to learn how to give myself fully to God, and understand that my work wasn't in vain. I had to train my mind to not look at what I was doing, but to look at WHO I was doing it for. This really helped me in learning how to just acknowledge God in my situations and let everything else come after that.*

Now, I want you to take some time and find 7 scriptures that will help you begin to change your perspective and train your mind to focus on God in ALL situations. Utilize your scriptures because its personal to you. Mine are personal to me, but I thought sharing my thoughts may be a little helpful to you as well.

1. Scripture: _____

_____

_____

_____

_____

_____

_____

PAIN. PROCESS. PURPOSE.

What made you choose this scripture?

2. Scripture:

PAIN.PROCESS.PURPOSE.

What made you choose this scripture?

3. Scripture: _____

PAIN. PROCESS. PURPOSE.

What made you choose this scripture?

4. Scripture:

PAIN.PROCESS.PURPOSE.

What made you choose this scripture?

5. Scripture: _____

PAIN.PROCESS.PURPOSE.

What made you choose this scripture?

6. Scripture:

PAIN.PROCESS.PURPOSE.

What made you choose this scripture?

7. Scripture:

PAIN . PROCESS . PURPOSE .

What made you choose this scripture?

PAIN. PROCESS. PURPOSE.

Remember that we should acknowledge the Lord not only by the way we live our lives, but by our thoughts as well. Even in the midst of our storms, we have to believe His promises and know that God will work in our lives!

3. Can you think of something that God has told you to do that you have not begun to do?

_____
_____
_____
_____
_____
_____
_____
_____
_____
_____
_____
_____
_____
_____
_____
_____
_____
_____

4. Do you feel that not committing to what God has told you to do is holding you back?

PAIN . PROCESS . PURPOSE .

One of the struggles I talk about in my book was "Obedience." I know for me, one of the things that God asked me to do was to remain celibate until marriage. That was a huge step in my growth with God. However, my step may not be the same as your step, but there is something that God is telling you do. God is always telling us things that will essentially help us in our process to our purpose, but sometimes we do not listen. I had a listening problem. I'm not suggesting that you do ☺, but I'm saying that I did. If you are one of those people, like me, that had a listening problem, I want you to focus on truly reaching to hear His voice.

Sometimes we are not obedient because we ignored what God told us to do. On the other side, sometimes we are not obedient because we failed to hear God. Our ear gates were so cluttered with nonsense that we couldn't hear the voice of the Lord. We couldn't decipher WHO was talking to us. To me, that feeling is worse than ignoring God. If you choose to ignore God, you had a choice, but if you don't know how to decipher His voice, that's not a choice. That means you never had the option to choose.

I'm going to share with you some of the verses that I researched and meditated on in order to start hearing God's voice and being obedient to God. Now, I know we did a similar exercise like this earlier, but most of the process is learning God, and learning how God operates with you.

I'm going to share with you 7 verses that I used to help me with learning to listen to God and obeying what God said. I will also share my reflections about each verse. After you have read through mine, I want you to do the same. This again will help you think about why you are obeying what God says, and not only that, spending time with God allows you to grow closer to Him. When you grow closer to Him, you are trained to decipher His Word from the enemy's deceit.

1. We are destroying sophisticated arguments and every exalted and proud thing that sets itself up against the [true] knowledge of God, and we are taking every thought and purpose captive to the obedience of Christ (2 Corinthians 10:5 AMP).

   My reflections: *This verse taught me that I needed to rid myself of every thought that didn't align with God. Sometimes, the very thing blocking us from hearing God and obeying Him, is the fact that we are clogging up our spirits with so much doubt and fear from the devil. We fill our hearts with situations we can't control, and we dwell on those more than we seek God. This taught me to take control over those thoughts and make them like Christ.*

2. For the word of God is living and active. Sharper than any double-edged sword, it penetrates even to dividing soul and spirit, joints and marrow; it judges the thoughts and attitudes of the heart. (Hebrews 4:12 ESV)

   My Reflections: *This verse was very clear to me. If you are going through a block where you truly can't hear God, the best thing to do is to dive deep into His word and listen. God is constantly talking to us. We just have to have the ears to listen. God's Word penetrates deep into us every time we read it, and the more we read His Word, the more we will be acquainted with Him.*

3. And this is love: that we walk in accordance with His commandments and are guided continually by His precepts. This is the commandment, just as you have heard from the beginning, that you should [always] walk in love. (2 John 1:6 AMP)

   My Reflections: *I know I talked about this in my book. God is Love. We should be a reflection of God all the time, and that means walking in love. Being obedient to God may not mean that we are doing things that make us "want to walk in love." However, I've learned that we have to walk in obedience to Him and His commands. All these things work together to push us into a closer relationship with God.*

4. All scripture is breathed out by God and profitable for teaching, for reproof, for correction, and for training in righteousness (2 Timothy 3:16 ESV)

   My Reflections: *It all leads back to spending time in God's Word. We have to have a love for God in order to hear God. God actually speaks through His Word. He speaks through thoughts, conversations, and many other circumstances. We will learn to hear God and be able to be obedient towards Him when we learn to use the channels He has given us to communicate with Him.*

5. But if you carefully obey his voice and do all that I say, then I will be an enemy to your enemies and an adversary to your adversaries. (Exodus 23:22 ESV)

   My Reflections: *Wow, God says if we obey Him, then he will be the enemy and adversary for us. I believe that obedience reaps all the rewards for us. We can't fight our battles alone, but we can fight our thoughts, flesh, or anything else that doesn't align with what God is telling us to do. When we do that, we are setting ourselves up for God to take on the same things we would have been fighting ourselves.*

6. If you are willing and obedient, you shall eat the good of the land. (Isaiah 1:19 ESV)

   My Reflections: *This verse is black and white and makes pure sense. If we choose to just be obedient, even if we don't agree with God in that moment, we shall reap a harvest. Just think about it. Everything we do in life affects everything. God could tell us to give the homeless guy $20 and we will not be obedient. But that could have been an angel in disguise that was waiting to bless someone showed him, and God could have wanted it for you, but we chose to not be obedient. Obedience is not just about being obedient to one thing. I know in my book the big thing was celibacy; however, there were a lot of little things I had to be obedient to as well. We are learning, but we are willing and obedient, we will eat the good of the land. That's powerful.*

7. But this command I gave them: "Obey my voice, and I will be your God, and you shall be my people. And walk in all the ways that I command you, that it may be well with you." (Jeremiah 7:23 ESV)

PAIN.PROCESS.PURPOSE.

My Reflections: *When we hear God's voice, it's imperative that we don't ignore Him. When we ignore God's voice and his commands, we take ourselves through things we never were intended to go through. That's what happened to me, and it happens to the best of us. But this verse assures us that we should obey His voice and His command, and all will be well with us. God has truly given us a way to be set for the rest of our lives, and although, it may seem like a small thing to ignore when we choose to ignore His voice. That small thing could be what opens the big doors, so choose to obey the voice of God.*

Now, I want you to take some time and find 7 scriptures that will help you begin to change your perspective on obedience. The goal is to find verses that you can relate to that will help guide you to remain close to God and be able to hear Him when He speaks to you. Utilize your scriptures because its personal to you. Mine are personal to me, but I thought sharing my thoughts may be a little helpful to you as well.

1. Scripture: _____

_____
_____
_____
_____
_____
_____
_____
_____

What made you choose this scripture?

_____
_____
_____
_____
_____
_____

PAIN . PROCESS . PURPOSE .

2. Scripture: _____

What made you choose this scripture?

PAIN.PROCESS.PURPOSE.

3. Scripture: _____

What made you choose this scripture?

PAIN. PROCESS. PURPOSE.

4. Scripture: _____

What made you choose this scripture?

PAIN. PROCESS. PURPOSE.

5. Scripture: _____

What made you choose this scripture?

PAIN. PROCESS. PURPOSE.

6. Scripture: _____

What made you choose this scripture?

PAIN. PROCESS. PURPOSE.

7. Scripture: _____

What made you choose this scripture?

I hope this exercise helped you think about ways that you can increase your submission to God. I hope it challenged you to see all the greatness that you can reap when you choose to be obedient to God. If you were blocked from hearing God, I pray that through this study and meditation on these scriptures you are breaking barriers. I pray that God is moving something on the inside of you and this process that you are going through will birth a major purpose in your life.

5. Do you spend time alone with God? If you do, what are some of things you do in your alone time with God?

_____
_____
_____
_____
_____
_____
_____
_____
_____
_____
_____
_____
_____
_____
_____
_____
_____
_____
_____
_____
_____
_____

PAIN. PROCESS. PURPOSE.

If you don't spend enough intimate time with God, or if you think you need some improvement (which we all do), let's do this next exercise.

On the left side of this chart, I want you to list your daily activities. I'm going to leave 15 blanks for you to type in things that you do from the time you wake up to the time you go to bed. After you have listed those 15 things, I want you to think about how much time you spend alone with God with no distractions. If the answer is not enough for you, lets correct it. (*Personal Note: I know I'm expecting Extreme Results in 2017-2018, and I know that requires extreme faith and extreme obedience. If I want to do that, the time I spend with God has to be multiplied* ☺, *so it's the same for you!*) Where in your schedule, do you see that you can add even an extra 5-10 minutes to read your Bible or talk with God?

Here's where it gets fun. On the right side, I want you to re-arrange your schedule and add the time in with God. That may mean that something has to get eliminated. That's okay. Isn't alone time with God more important? Let's try this exercise!

1. _____	1. _____
2. _____	2. _____
3. _____	3. _____
4. _____	4. _____
5. _____	5. _____
6. _____	6. _____
7. _____	7. _____
8. _____	8. _____
9. _____	9. _____
10. _____	10. _____
11. _____	11. _____
12. _____	12. _____
13. _____	13. _____
14. _____	14. _____
15. _____	15. _____

6. What can you do today to push yourself to another level in your relationship with God? Be honest with yourself and God!

7. How can you implement the things that you can do today to push you to another level with God? And when are you going to implement these things? *Remember in order to progress, you have to put into action the things that you are learning. Let's hold you accountable today!*

8. Have you taken the time to ask God what He wants for your life? Take some time to really think about this, and if you have asked God, what are some of the things He wants for your life?

PAIN.PROCESS.PURPOSE.

PAIN. PROCESS. PURPOSE.

9. Now that you know what God wants for your life, are you ready to start chasing your purpose?

PAIN. PROCESS. PURPOSE.

Before you go on to start chasing your purpose. Please write 10 goals that God has placed in your heart to achieve! Remember to set a date for completion!

1. Goal: _____

_____

_____

_____

2. Goal: _____

_____

_____

_____

3. Goal: _____

_____

_____

_____

4. Goal: _____

_____

_____

_____

5. Goal: _____

_____

_____

_____

PAIN.PROCESS.PURPOSE.

6. Goal: _____

_____

_____

_____

7. Goal: _____

_____

_____

_____

8. Goal: _____

_____

_____

_____

9. Goal: _____

_____

_____

_____

10. Goal: _____

_____

_____

_____

PAIN . PROCESS . PURPOSE .

Yayyy! I'm sure going through this was definitely a process, but the best thing about it is that your purpose is right around the corner. You are growing closer and closer to God each and every day. Don't stop with these exercises, make some of your own. These were ways I grew closer to God, but you may have your own methods and I definitely want you to apply them. Take some time now and just meditate on the verses you did write. Take some time to pray and prepare your mind for the next section. Thank God for your process because it was and is continually vital in making you who you are. As mentioned before, remember the back of the book has your "Thank You Journal" in it. Remember to consistently thank God for the small things He is doing in your process every day.

I have also left some space here for you to write freely about your process.

MY PERSONAL THOUGHTS...

PAIN. PROCESS. PURPOSE.

PAIN. PROCESS. PURPOSE.

PAIN. PROCESS. PURPOSE.

PAIN. PROCESS. PURPOSE.

PAIN. PROCESS. PURPOSE.

PAIN. PROCESS. PURPOSE.

PURPOSE

Let's talk about purpose. Purpose is and will always be ongoing. The goal is to get in right alignment with God to continue to chase your God-intended purpose. God creates different purposes for us as we grow in Him. He gives us different assignments that are specifically hand spun for us. As you think about your pain and your process, you will notice that a lot of those things happened because it was preparing you for something greater within your purpose. In my book, there were things with my father that happened in pain and process that I needed to go through to be prepared for my purpose. My "love" life went through its own pain and process and God used that lesson to prepare me for the love life in my purpose. The list could go on. God is always with us during the different stages in our lives, and even when it is rough, I believe that God is still working it out for our good. Our purpose was designed for us. We all have gifts and in Proverbs 18:16, the Bible says. "your gifts will make room for you." God is continually opening doors and making room for us to use the God given gifts that He has given us. Although your pain and process was hard, God graced you with the ability to be able to not just get through your situations, but to conquer them. It all comes full circle. Your pain had to take place to put you in a place to process it with God, and that pain is going to help lead you into your purpose. That hard time that you went through is going to be the very thing that plants a seed in you to manifest into something great. Honestly, this book would have never been completed if God wouldn't have taken me through the pain of losing my dad. It birthed something in me that took me through a process, and led me to a purpose that was bigger than me. I'm sharing my story in hopes that it blesses as many people that pick it up. That was something that was birthed from a seed that I thought would break me. What the devil thought was bad, God turned it around and made it for good. If He did it for me, trust and believe, He will also do it for you! I'm excited that we have made it to the purpose section! Let's conquer it!

Love Always,
Chanel Chase

1. What is keeping you from pursuing your God given purpose?

_____
_____
_____
_____
_____
_____
_____
_____

PAIN. PROCESS. PURPOSE.

PAIN.PROCESS.PURPOSE.

For me, it was FEAR! If you wrote about that, I completely understand and can relate to that. In my book, I talked about how I didn't want to be different. I didn't want to stand out. I want you to remember 1 Timothy 1:7, "For God has not given you the spirit of fear, but of power, love, and a sound mind." Fear cannot stop you from pursuing your purpose. The only person in the world you should reverently fear is God. Other than that, no one can come close or near to you. I want you to remember that as you push on in to your purpose. You can do it, and whatever you wrote that is keeping you from getting there, LET IT GO NOW!!!!

2. Have you evaluated your relationships based on what God wants for your life?

_____
_____
_____
_____
_____
_____
_____
_____
_____
_____
_____
_____
_____
_____
_____
_____
_____
_____
_____
_____
_____
_____
_____

PAIN . PROCESS . PURPOSE .

OK! So, this is a really HUGE one! Friendships and relationships are the hardest things to let go of, especially if you are forming any type of bond. But please evaluate the bond and see if it was given to you by God. Sometimes we create what we want to work. In my previous relationship, I created what I wanted to work, and we see where that left me.

Right now, I want to try an exercise. In life, we have a "Holy of Holies", an inner court, and an outer court. We are going to evaluate the people that are in your holy of holies and see if your relationships are aligning with God. I want you to list the person's name at the top and I want you to write how that relationships aligns with God. *I challenge you to ask that person to evaluate their feelings toward the relationship as well.* God wants our relationships to flourish and align with His Word. I will provide some verses, and as you evaluate the friendships and relationships, see if they align with the same characteristics. I will also leave you room to write your own verses as well.

Walk with the wise and become wise, for a companion of fools suffers harm. (Proverbs 13:20)

Greater love has no one than this; to lay down one's life for one's friends. (John 15:13)

Be completely humble and gentle; be patient, bearing with one another in love. Make every effort to keep the unity of the Spirit through the bond of peace. (Ephesians 4:2-3)

A friend loves at all times, and a brother is born for adversity. (Proverbs 17:17)

Do not bound together with unbelievers; for what partnership have righteousness and lawlessness, or what fellowship has light with darkness. (2 Corinthians 6:14)

Do not associate with a man given to anger; or go with a hot-tempered man, or you will learn his ways and find a snare for yourself. (Proverbs 22:24-25)

Iron sharpens iron, so one man sharpens another. (Proverbs 27:17)

One who has unreliable friends soon comes to ruin, but there is a friend who sticks closer than a brother. (Proverbs 18:24)

One who is righteous is a guide to his neighbor, but the way of the wicked leads them astray. (Proverbs 12:26)

A scoffer seeks wisdom in vain, but knowledge is easy for a man of understanding. Leave the presence of a fool, for there you do not meet words of knowledge. (Proverbs 14:6-7)

Listen to advice and accept instruction, that you may gain wisdom in the future. (Proverbs 19:20)

PAIN. PROCESS. PURPOSE.

Now you can find some verses on your own:

1. _____

2. _____

3. _____

4. _____

PAIN. PROCESS. PURPOSE.

5.

6.

7.

PAIN. PROCESS. PURPOSE.

Now Let's talk about your "Holy of Holies." This group of people should be people that you trust the most. It's a place of *intimacy behind the veil,* and it's your most intimate place in friendships and relationships. You should take these friendships and relationships very seriously, and it is very important that they align with God. They should be the friends that aren't afraid to celebrate and encourage you. They are the friends that will also give you your constructive criticism.

Here is where you will evaluate the relationships in your life. It seems silly, but it's not. In my book, I talked about having to separate from people, and so much more. I had to separate because they didn't align with my purpose. Doing this little exercise will show who should be in your Holy of Holies because those are the people that will help you on your journey to your purpose.

1. Friend: _____

How does this friendship/relationship align with God?

_____
_____
_____
_____
_____
_____
_____

2. Friend: _____

How does this friendship/relationship align with God?

_____
_____
_____
_____
_____
_____
_____

PAIN.PROCESS.PURPOSE.

3. Friend: _____

How does this friendship/relationship align with God?

_____
_____
_____
_____
_____
_____
_____

4. Friend: _____

How does this friendship/relationship align with God?

_____
_____
_____
_____
_____
_____
_____

5. Friend: _____

How does this friendship/relationship align with God?

_____
_____
_____
_____
_____
_____

PAIN . PROCESS . PURPOSE .

I hope your evaluation of your *Holy of Holies* helped clarify that your friendships and relationships are in alignment with God. If not, pray for friendships and relationships that will help guide you closer to your God-intended purpose.

3. How has my journey related to the journey that you are getting ready to embark on?

_____
_____
_____
_____
_____
_____
_____
_____
_____
_____
_____
_____
_____
_____
_____
_____
_____
_____
_____
_____
_____
_____
_____
_____

CHANEL CHASE

PAIN. PROCESS. PURPOSE.

4. How has your process changed you?

PAIN.PROCESS.PURPOSE.

5. How can you use your journey to help others get to where they need to be? Remember that your test can become someone else's testimony!

_____
_____
_____
_____
_____
_____
_____
_____
_____
_____
_____
_____
_____
_____
_____
_____
_____
_____
_____
_____
_____
_____
_____
_____

PAIN . PROCESS . PURPOSE .

6. What do you feel is the higher calling for your life?

PAIN. PROCESS. PURPOSE.

PAIN. PROCESS. PURPOSE.

7. What do you feel like God is leading you to do?

PAIN. PROCESS. PURPOSE.

PAIN. PROCESS. PURPOSE.

8. What do you need to do today to get back on track towards your purpose?

PAIN . PROCESS . PURPOSE .

These all were some really deep and compelling questions that were meant to help push you to a new level. I know that they have probably challenged your mind to think beyond what you were expecting! That's great! Your purpose is determined for greatness!

I have one more exercise. We have to end this on a positive note. I want you to think of 10 P words that are going to help PUSH you into your next level of purpose. Since the book is focusing on P's, I wanted to keep that going. I'm going to give you 5 of my words and then I want you to create 10 Positive Words that will push you into your purpose!

MY P WORDS....
1. Powerful
2. Passionate
3. Personal Growth
4. Progressively
5. Prosperous

Now you give it a try!

1. _____
2. _____
3. _____
4. _____
5. _____
6. _____
7. _____
8. _____
9. _____
10. _____

These words are your POWER WORDS FOR PURPOSE! Speak them into your life Daily!!!!!

PAIN. PROCESS. PURPOSE.

9. Are you ready to continue CHASING YOUR PURPOSE? ITS YOUR TIME! BE INTENTIONAL WITH YOUR GOD GIVEN PURPOSE!

PAIN . PROCESS . PURPOSE .

YOU CAN! YOU WILL!! YOU ARE DESTINED FOR GREATNESS!

As you read those questions, I pray that you truly journaled and pin pointed areas in your journey where you can make a positive turn in the direction of your purpose. I pray that my journey allowed you to see that we all have situations that we must learn to deal with and that no one's life is perfect. I pray that you can identify the painful moments in life and ask God to heal those open wounds. As you go through the process, I pray that you are learning step-by- step what God intends for your life. Evaluate your friendships, your relationships, and your everyday encounters with people to make sure that you are keeping them in line with God. I pray that from this process, God reveals to you your purpose and that every day you are fulfilling your God given purpose. Your journey will be the imprint that you leave on this earth! I pray that you are allowing God to use you in every way possible. As mentioned before, remember the back of the book has your "Thank You Journal" in it. Remember to consistently thank God for the small things he is doing as He leads you into your purpose!

I'm going to leave you some blank pages so you can just journal before you move on.

I love you! God Bless!

If you need prayer, please feel free to get on the Wisdom Inspiration Celebration Prayer Call daily at 6:30 AM EST. Call: 641-715-3690 pin code: 920910#

MY PERSONAL THOUGHTS…

_____
_____
_____
_____
_____
_____
_____
_____
_____
_____
_____

CHANEL CHASE

PAIN.PROCESS.PURPOSE.

PAIN. PROCESS. PURPOSE.

PAIN. PROCESS. PURPOSE.

PAIN. PROCESS. PURPOSE.

PAIN. PROCESS. PURPOSE.

PAIN. PROCESS. PURPOSE.
THANK YOU JOURNAL

PAIN. PROCESS. PURPOSE.

PAIN. PROCESS. PURPOSE.

PAIN. PROCESS. PURPOSE.

PAIN. PROCESS. PURPOSE.

PAIN . PROCESS . PURPOSE .

PAIN. PROCESS. PURPOSE.

PAIN. PROCESS. PURPOSE.

PAIN. PROCESS. PURPOSE.

PAIN. PROCESS. PURPOSE.

PAIN. PROCESS. PURPOSE.

PAIN. PROCESS. PURPOSE.

PAIN. PROCESS. PURPOSE.

PAIN. PROCESS. PURPOSE.

PAIN. PROCESS. PURPOSE.

PAIN. PROCESS. PURPOSE.

PAIN. PROCESS. PURPOSE.

PAIN. PROCESS. PURPOSE.

PAIN.PROCESS.PURPOSE.

PAIN. PROCESS. PURPOSE.

PAIN.PROCESS.PURPOSE.

Let's Keep in Contact

Website: www.pain2purposebook.com

@pain2purposebook

Page: fb.me/pain2purposebook
Group: Pain Process Purpose

pain2purposebk

info@pain2purposebook.com

Book Me for Your Next Event:
info@chanelchase.com

PAIN.PROCESS.PURPOSE.

CHANEL CHASE